SMALL STEPS for BIG CHANGE

JUMBO COLOURING Book

FIVE MILE

Did You Know?

Most of the food we eat start as flowers?

Cool Colours

Fill this mandala in with blues and greens!

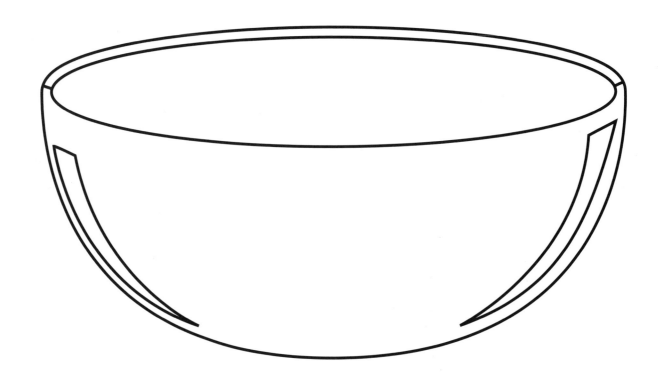

Eat Healthy

Draw your favourite fruits in the bowl!

Orange

Red

Food Colours

Colour in the pictures above to make a food rainbow!

Favourite Vegetables

Add some of your favourite
veggies to the bowl below!

Stretch

Reach toward your toes!

Meditate

Relax, and start to take some deep breaths in and out.

I Love to Read

Create a cover for your favourite book below!

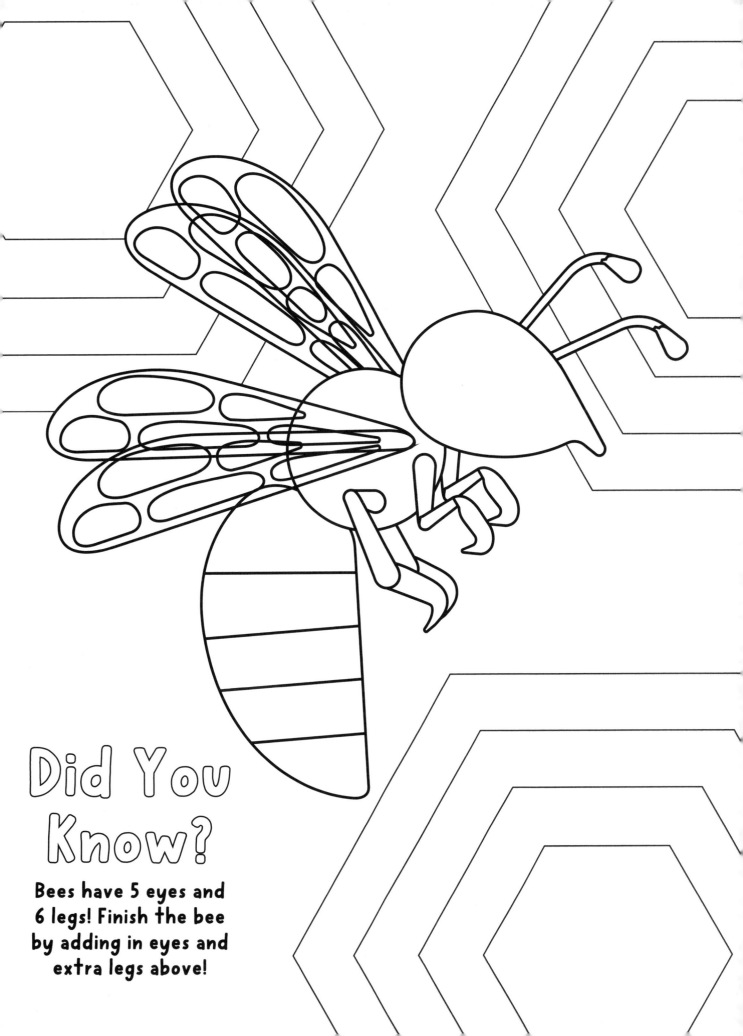

Did You Know?

Bees have 5 eyes and 6 legs! Finish the bee by adding in eyes and extra legs above!

Did You Know?

There are around 10,000 species of birds!

Colour by Number

Use the key to colour in the butterfly!

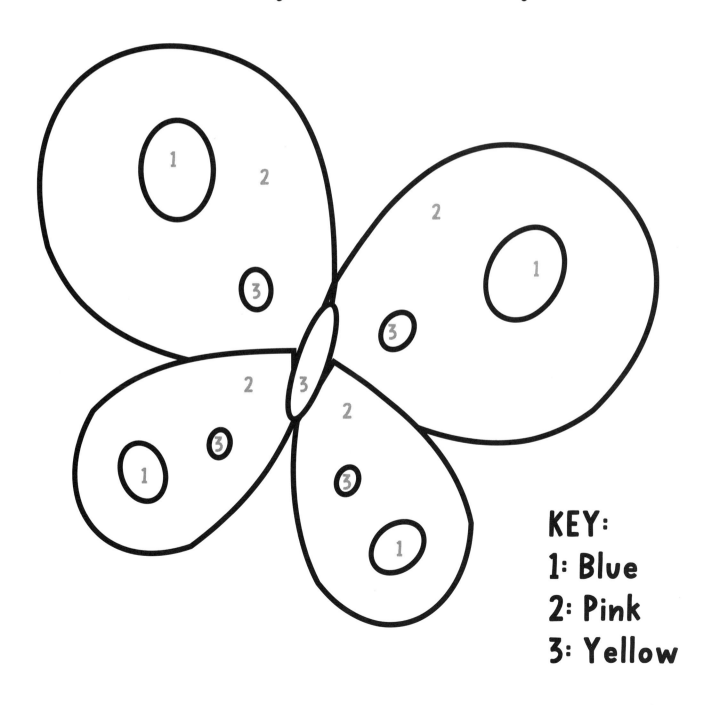

KEY:
1: Blue
2: Pink
3: Yellow

Yoga

Stretch your arms above your head
and place your hands together.

Grateful

Draw what you are grateful for in the hearts below.

JOURNAL YOUR DAY

Journalling is one of the best ways to express yourself. Start by writing what you did and how you felt during the day.

Paint Your Feelings

Painting is a great way to express yourself! Use your favourite colours to paint how you feel.

Time to

Relax!

Recycle

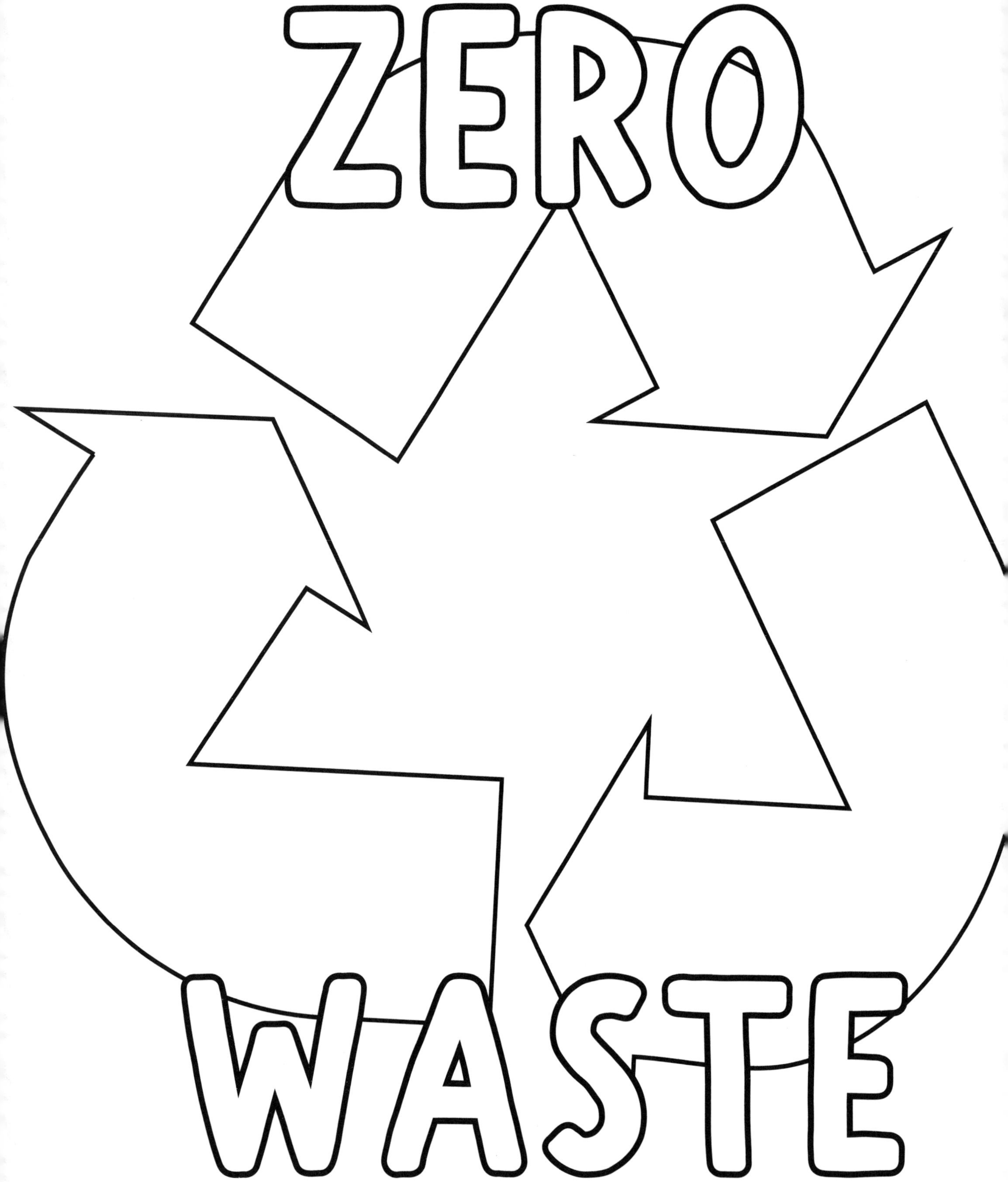
ZERO
WASTE

COMPOST

Did You Know?

You can compost almost all of your household waste!